Komodo Dragons! Facts About Komodo Dragons

TERRY MASON

Copyright © 2017 Terry Mason
All rights reserved.
ISBN-13:978-1977504593

WHAT IS A KOMODO DRAGON

A Komodo dragon is a kind of lizard. In fact it is the biggest lizard in the world today, and also the heaviest. It is a reptilian animal, which means that it is a reptile. A reptile is a cold blooded creature that usually has scaly skin. Lizards, snakes and crocodiles are reptilian animals.

Komodo Dragons have been compared to the mythological dragon because of their fearsome appearance; large flat head with long rounded snout and a long forked yellow tongue.

Their scales are hard and their claws are sharp. They look more like wingless dragons than huge lizards and have the ability to capture their prey either through powerful bite attacks or poison.
Komodo dragons are the only living creature that has these specific set of abilities and there are only few left in the world, isolated in the Komodo Islands.

KOMODO DRAGON FACTS

A komodo dragon has a scaly body with bony plates like other reptiles and has a set of 60 sharp teeth that are serrated, meaning having jagged edges. Each tooth is at least 1 inch long.

Behavior

Komodo dragons are mostly solitary animals, meaning they live and hunt on their own. They join in packs sometimes when it is time to find a mate or someplace to lay eggs. A group of komodo dragons will also gather around a kill, even if it belongs to another predator.

Komodo dragons have a habit of rubbing their body and tummy on the carcass of animals. Younger komodo dragons show this habit more often than adults. They rub their bodies on either the guts of the dead animals or the hair.

Younger komodo dragons do this to protect themselves from larger predators. The smell of the feces or poop of the dead animal hides their own smell. It is also believed that the smell of something rotting drives the predators away quickly.

Mating

There are more female komodo dragons than males one. For every male komodo dragon there are four female komodo dragons. Both become mature at around 8 to 10 years. The female komodo dragon lays around 12 to 30 eggs at a time.

Male komodo dragons will compete for a female's attention. They will do this by wrestling with each other and even rearing themselves up on their thick tails to claw at each other.

How Komodo Dragons Grow

Komodo dragons mate in the summer sometime in May and June. Female komodo dragons will lay their eggs later in July and August in a shallow pit-like nest. The eggs will incubate or develop for 9 months before they start hatching.

WHAT DO KOMODO DRAGONS LOOK LIKE

A Komodo dragon looks a lot like a lizard, except bigger and more muscular. It crawls on all fours with bowed legs and a muscular tail. Its head is wide and flat with a rounded snout, making it look like a dragon. It also has a very long snake-like tongue that is yellow and flicks in and out of the mouth.

Its Body and Color

It has a scaly body that is often grayish brown. Some komodo dragons are brown red in color with yellowish heads and the younger ones have skin patterns. Their skins have different bands or speckles; some have yellow or greens speckles while others have either brown or gray bands.

How Big It Is

An adult komodo dragon can measure as long as 10 feet or 3 meters and weigh at around 70 kilograms, but some get as heavy as 140 kilograms! It looks like a slow animal because it likes to sleep a lot, but it can suddenly sprint and run as fast as 20 kilometers per hour or 12 miles per hour.

WHERE DO KOMODO DRAGONS LIVE

Wild komodo dragons live in Indonesia, in the Lesser Sunda Islands of Komodo, more known as the Komodo Islands. These islands are:

•Rinca

•Komodo

•Gili Dasami

•Gili Montag

•and the Flores Islands

Scientists believe that Komodo Dragons originally lived in Australia, based on several fossil findings. Research shows that they migrated over 400 million years ago from Australia to different islands to the west in search of food and mating grounds.

THE KOMODO DRAGON HOME

Their habitat or place where the komodo dragons make their home is usually volcanic. This means it is close to a volcano. They also mostly live in dry places like the desert and savannas.

Burrowing

They like to burrow holes in the ground where they sleep and keep the heat preserved. Komodo dragons also dig up a shallow pit to lay their eggs in the summer.

Shelter and Safety

Baby komodo dragons are only 12 inches long when hatched from the eggs. They are not cared for by their mother and so are in danger of bird and larger animals that eat meat. They often need to climb trees to keep safe. They will feed on or hunt lizards, rats and also snakes.

They will stop living in trees and start spending more time on the ground when they are around 4 feet long or around 4 years of age. A komodo dragon can live up to more than 30 years, some reaching 50 years old.

THE KOMODO DRAGON'S SENSES

The komodo dragons have very poor hearing. Its ears are holes that can easily be seen at the sides of its head. Komodo dragons are not deaf but can only hear low frequencies at a time, so they don't rely on hearing when catching prey.

The komodo dragons rely on its sense of smell to tell if a prey is nearby. They can smell prey and even carcasses as far as 5 kilometers away.

Instead of just its nose, a komodo dragon also uses its tongue to catch the scent of other animals. Its tongue flicks in and out of its mouth a lot to taste the air. It is able to catch small particles that, when tasted, gives them information about its surroundings.

Its mouth is very venomous which means its saliva is poisonous. There are over 50 types of bacteria found in a komodo dragon's saliva. It is almost like the venom of a snake except it enters into the victim's body through the wound. The prey poisoned by the komodo dragon's saliva goes into shock or dies of blood loss.

WHAT KOMODO DRAGONS EAT

Komodo dragons eat meat. Their favorite animals to hunt are deer and the water buffalo. These animals may be bigger in size but the komodo dragons are able to consume a lot of meat.

Hunting

The komodo dragon's diet includes almost all types of animals found in the island like monkeys, goats, wild boars and horses. They may be able to kill birds occasionally but often feed on a dead bird's body.

They also like to hunt pigs and other smaller prey. In fact, in the islands that the komodo dragons live they are on the top of the food chain. This means there are no animals in those islands that hunt the adult komodo dragons.

While still young, komodo dragons rely on smaller animals to feed on. They may eat birds' or snakes' eggs and even hunt geckos and insects. They are both scavengers and hunters, and will eat almost anything as long as it is meat.

Scavenging

Komodo dragons can hunt their own prey but will also eat leftovers of a different predator. They can smell carcasses from miles away and will even eat meat that is several weeks old. This adds up to the bacteria and poison in their saliva.

Komodo dragons rarely leave leftovers and are hearty eaters. They can gnaw at and swallow a whole pig in minutes. Unfortunately, they can only eat 10 to 12 meals a day because their metabolism is slow. Metabolism means the ability to digest food in the stomach. The slower the animal's metabolism is the longer it feels full and unable to eat again.

THE KOMODO DRAGON FAMILY

History

Komodo dragons come from the same animals that the dinosaurs came from. However, they are not related with the dinosaurs or descend from them even though they look like it. The first specie related with the komodo dragon lived over a hundred million years ago.

Scientists believe that the komodo dragons today evolved from a second line of lizard species that lived 4 million years ago. These lizards were also very big and lived in Australia. Scientists believe that they migrated to the western islands and evolved a little more there.

Why They Are Large

In those islands also lived the Pygmy Elephants or Stegodon. In order for the komodo dragons to hunt and survive from these elephant they had to evolve into larger lizards. The islands that the komodo dragons migrated to are what is now known as the Komodo islands of Indonesia.

Discovery

The first officially documented komodo dragon sighting was by Lieutenant van Steyn van Hensbroek in 1910. He heard many stories about giant lizards from the locals and so traveled to the Komodo Islands. When he came to the island he hunted down the said giant lizard and killed it.

Lieutenant van Steyn van Hoensbroek sent the skin of the so-called dragon along with photographs to the director of the Zoological Museum and Botanical Garden in Bogor, Java. The person who received the sample and photographs was Peter A. Quwens. From that skin sample, he was able to determine that the animal was a monitor Lizard.

KOMODO DRAGONS IN CAPTIVITY

There are around 30 American zoos that have komodo dragons in captivity. On average, they can only live up to 25 years compared to the wild komodo dragons that live for more than 30 years, sometimes up to 50 years.

Komodo dragons can easily be tamed when captured. They somehow have a gentle side. They can recognize their caretakers and follow them everywhere, like begging for food or just sniffing around. Komodo dragons will often ignore people they do not know, even during feeding hours.

All in all, komodo dragons in zoos have a good temperament and develop a liking for their keepers.

WHEN KOMODO DRAGONS ATTACK

Komodo dragons are not the fastest predators and they have a funny way of walking too. However, they are very good at hiding themselves to blend with their surroundings, this is called camouflaging.

When a komodo dragon hunts, it doesn't follow its prey. Instead, it hides and camouflages itself and wait for a victim to pass by. When an opportunity comes, it will attack the prey by rearing itself up with its thick, muscular tail.

It will then bite the prey with its sharp teeth and wound with its long claws. It can shred its prey to death because its teeth is almost like a shark's; sharp and serrated.

When a komodo dragon is able to bite or wound its prey that animal can be considered dead. Even if the prey escapes the komodo dragon's teeth it eventually dies because of poisoning from the komodo dragon's saliva. The prey won't survive for more than 24 hours of being bitten.

FUN FACTS ABOUT KOMODO DRAGONS

Komodo dragons have a clumsy way of walking. They walk back and forth and have difficulty in turning.

Komodo dragons can swim! They are actually good at it and can have a dip in the open sea. They can swim from one island to another to find prey or a mate.

Komodo dragons can eat a lot in one meal, as much as 80% of their own body weight.

Komodo dragons have excellent vision. They can see anything that is as far as 300 meters or 985 feet away.

When a komodo dragon walks, its head and tail sways from side to side making it look like it is listening to a beat.

COMPREHENSION TEST

Komodo dragons are not always successful in killing their prey with their bite attacks but it still manages to kill and feed on it within the day. How is this possible?

1. Can Komodo dragons swim?

2. Are Komodo dragons descendants of dinosaurs?

3. How many bacteria can be found in the Komodo dragon's mouth?

4. How long can a Komodo dragon live?

The answers are found in the back of the book

MORE PICTURES

COMPREHENSION TEST ANSWER

The prey dies in 24 hours from the komodo dragon's bite because of the poison and bacteria in its saliva. It dies from blood loss and the komodo dragon can track it by smell from 5 kilometers away.

1. Yes, they are great swimmers.

2. No, they are not. They evolved from the same animals that the dinosaurs came from but are not direct descendant of dinosaur.

3 There are 50 types of bacteria found in its mouth.

4. A komodo dragon can live between 30 and 50 years.

Manufactured by Amazon.ca
Bolton, ON